Australian S
Complete Guide

The Basic Information for Correctly Feeding and Grooming
Your Aussie from Puppyhood to Seniority

By

Polly Saunders

Table of Contents

Introduction

Buying and bringing an Australian Shepherd home is the best way to build a friendship with a wonderful dog and thus live a unique and unrepeatable experience.

The Australian Shepherd, also called Aussie, is an intelligent, hardworking animal capable of performing many different tasks.

He is a versatile and strong dog that needs the necessary space to carry out the daily physical exercises; moreover, he always seeks attention from his master, reciprocating with great affection.

The Australian Shepherd is a typical farm dog who loves to work; this fantastic buddy is agile, animated, and adaptable to all situations. The Australian Shepherd is very good at obeying and has a real sense of purpose.

Agility, herding trials, and discipline are the fields in which the Aussie excels.

These dogs are affectionate, lively, protective, courageous, and efficient for housekeeping. They are intelligent and easy to train, have a docile and quiet character, and love to please their master; they are considered "human" animals because they love to spend time with their family.

They may get upset a little when they first meet a stranger.

This guide will help you train your Australian Shepherd, regardless of age and physical size. It will make you understand the dog's attitudes, assigning you the right role towards him.

The book covers all the fundamental aspects of training a dog: the things to do, the things to avoid, the basic training commands, the leash, the creation of restricted areas, and other important activities to be carried out.

Once you have read the entire book, you can calmly face your dog's most dangerous actions, such as biting, digging, jumping, dragging, eating harmful objects, chasing other animals, and many more.

You will therefore feel that you have taken a crash course in training for your Australian Shepherd.

CHAPTER 1: The Australian Shepherd

Even before purchasing an Australian Shepherd, you must understand the breed's characteristics and plan its training in detail to have the best possible behavior in any situation.

Since Australian Shepherds change their way of behaving very often during the stages of growth, it becomes essential to understand these fluctuations in temperament in advance to carry out training and grooming in the best possible way.

1.1 History and origins of the Australian Shepherd

This breed most likely developed in the Pyrenees Mountains between France and Spain and was perfected in the western United States, working on ranches as herding dogs from the early 30s of the 9th centuries, in the famous period of the race gold.

Unfortunately, even if called in this way, the Australian Shepherd is not Australian, having created a misunderstanding over the decades about the origin of the name.

The ancestors of the Australian Shepherd were Spanish dogs used by Basque shepherds to watch over the sheep that would later be sold to America and Australia.

After a few years, this breed crossed with the Collie strain, changing the name several times: **Pastor Dog**, **Blue Heeler**, **New American Shepherd**, **California Shepherd**, **Spanish Shepherd**. Among this breed's many talents, consider recovery, detection of narcotics, guarding, herding, search and rescue, agility, tricks, and competitive obedience.

1.2 Character and behavioral aspects

The Australian Shepherd is intelligent and dedicated to working with excellent skills as a keeper and Shepherd. It is flexible and can easily train, performing the assigned tasks with passion and dedication.

He could become your best friend even if, amid strangers, he might seem aloof and cold; moreover, he has a lower tolerance if the people or animals around him behave aggressively.

This breed is used to struggling and helping its owner in any extreme or difficult situation.

1.2.1 An excellent company

Australian Shepherds always want to know what you want from them and are happy to obey your commands - they are the best friends you could ever want and are protective by nature.

If they are working as cattle dogs, they change strategies according to their handler's actual needs; they feel sad if they do not achieve their goals or if they carry out activities that are not useful to the will of the master.

They are very determined, and if problems or injuries occur at work, they recover in a short time, managing to work even in extreme conditions.

When you feel that your Australian Shepherd has been seriously injured, you must look into the problem and treat him.

1.2.2 A hard worker

The Australian Shepherd must be physically and mentally motivated. That is, there must be a healthy balance connected to this aspect. Otherwise, problems could arise.

For the Aussie, solving problems is fundamental for his personality and is a constant stimulus to improve; he loves challenges and feels fulfilled whenever he solves a problem.

Unfortunately, many owners offer their Australian Shepherd the necessary physical exercise but fail to give sufficient mental motivation to improve the puppy's growth.

1.2.3 Cunning and intelligence

The intelligence of this breed is very high and can be immediately noticed through their independent thought process and problem-solving techniques.

The Australian Shepherd is optimistic and ready to emerge in any situation, working excellently with livestock and other essential roles.

As an Aussie owner, you should carefully teach your puppy his limits before introducing them to take advantage of his abilities.

1.2.4 The best leader

For a long time, Australian shepherd breeders have been reported to have the ability to command cattle with firmness. The Australian Shepherd is by nature a leader and manages to have considerable influence, keeping things in order.

So, even in the most challenging times, Australian Shepherds can confidently fulfill their leading role.

1.3 Physical characteristics

1.3.1 Lifespan

The life of an Australian Shepherd ranges from 11 to 14 years, but it is common for him to live up to 16 years, as long as he does not develop serious health problems first.

1.3.2 Color and physical appearance

The color of the Australian Shepherd can be black, blue merle, red merle, and red. The Australian Shepherd can also be solid and have white markings or tan spots, depending on the genes.

The hair can be upright or undulating and medium length; it is usually short around the ears, front of legs, and head.

1.3.3 Main features

Below you will have an overview of the main characteristics of the Australian Shepherd:

1) adaptability;
2) friendship for the family;
3) ease of grooming;
4) playfulness;
5) intelligence.

1.3.4 Weight and height

An adult Australian shepherd is 19 to 24 inches tall at the shoulder and weighs 45 to 70 pounds, depending on its traits.

CHAPTER 2: Choose your Australian Shepherd

2.1 Contact a serious breeder

The Australian Shepherd breed is rare, and finding a serious and recommended breeder could be tricky; you may have to go far to find a breeder who has the Australian Shepherd you want because maybe there are no breeding farms near your home.

On the other hand, you could also receive your Aussie directly by courier. In this case, first, you will be placed on a waiting list, and then the puppy will be delivered to you. You need to be patient. Even if the wait may seem frustrating, it will be worth it.

A severe breeder must have health clearances for each dog he owns.

The following are the health clearances required in the United States:

- OFA evaluation by a recognized laboratory;
- hip dysplasia;
- elbow dysplasia;
- eye examination;
- autoimmune thyroid (optional);
- multiple drug sensitivity;
- results registered at the CERF;
- eye anomaly.

On the following pages, you will be able to learn about other fundamental requirements that your breeder must possess.

2.1.1 Good references

The breeder you choose must have excellent references. Therefore, you must inform yourself well about the references possessed by your breeder and if you are not convinced of his professionalism, look for another breeder.

2.1.2 Dog health

You must check that the dogs owned by the breeder are in good health. Mothers nursing a large litter look rough and may lose weight and hair, but that would be completely normal.

2.1.3 Cleaning of the facilities

The place and facilities where Australian Shepherds are kept must be clean. The breeder must always allow you to see his breeding; otherwise, choose another one.

If the breeder has very young puppies under four weeks of age, he may refuse to show you the kennel for fear that fatal diseases will be introduced and transmitted to the puppies.

2.1.4 Documentations

You must request paperwork and documentation relating to dogs. The breeder must have registration documents, dog purchase contracts, certifications, health authorizations, and information on the family tree.

Make sure that the breeder you are contacting has all these documents.

Although the Australian Shepherd is happy outdoors, it is advisable for his health and socialization that he be raised indoors. You will have significant benefits if you can raise your pet indoors.

2.2 How to choose your Australian Shepherd

After selecting the breeder and the Australian Shepherd litter is born, you must choose the right puppy.

Breeders often help you choose the right puppy for you as they have years of experience and know a puppy's temperament and character well. The most experienced breeders manage to match puppies to their owners perfectly.

You can choose between different puppies, different kinds, and different colors. Let the breeder understand which puppy would be most suitable for you. If you want a show dog, get one with the typical temperament and characteristics of the standard breed dog.

If you want a pet dog, don't worry about the breed standard requirements, but choose a puppy of any color and gender. If you want an obedient and agile herding dog, inform the breeder who will be able to give you the right dog for you in terms of intelligence and temperament.

After making the first choice as to which type of Australian Shepherd you want, spend some time watching the puppies play and have fun together.

Avoid getting a shy puppy or one that remains isolated because when he becomes an adult, he will have excellent temperament and behavioral problems.

When choosing your Australian Shepherd, you need to look at temperament, health, and several important characteristics.

2.2.1 Excellent physical conditions

Carefully observe the physical conditions of the puppy you want to take and those of his coat.

In addition to being thick and soft, the hair must not have dandruff, dullness, or crunchy areas. The torso needs to be wide enough that you don't need to see the ribs but still lean enough to feel them when you touch them.

2.2.2 Brightness of the eyes

Your Aussie's eyes must be bright, shiny, and lively. They must have no secretions and must have no debris. Don't choose a lethargic puppy; if you arrive at the kennel during nap time, wait for the puppies to be awake to be able to observe the characteristics of their eyes well.

2.2.3 Nose, sight, and hearing

The Australian Shepherd must have a moist, shiny nose and must not exhibit breathing problems.

As for sight and hearing, clap your hands hard and convince the puppy to chase the toys. Observe his reaction and if you see that he cannot hear or see, choose another puppy.

2.3 The ways to buy your Australian Shepherd

You can purchase your Australian Shepherd from a breeder, pet store, or rescue service.

2.3.1 The breeder

As mentioned earlier, getting a dog from a breeder is undoubtedly the best way because you will be able to interact with the puppy before buying it.

You will be able to understand the character and behavior of the dog, and you will be able to inspect it to know if it has obvious genetic defects.

Contact breeders who are part of a registered organization, so you will be sure to rely on a qualified and responsible person. Additionally, breeders will be able to alert you to any dog problems, how they have socialized it, and will be able to tell you your puppy's exact date of birth.

The downside of buying a dog from a breeder is the cheap one, as they are more expensive than pet shops. However, spending doesn't have to be a problem if you want to buy a dog.

2.3.2 Pet shop

Many people buy their new dog at a pet store that almost always buys dogs directly from puppy breeders.

However, pet shop employees don't often know specific information about the dogs they sell, such as date of birth or health condition.

2.3.3 Rescue service

If you already have experience in buying a dog, you could get a dog from a rescue service.

Most of these facilities are accessible, requiring only a donation. Dogs taken to rescue services could have health or character problems due to the discomfort they have lived in for a long time; furthermore, they are not puppies but are middle-aged or even elderly dogs.

If you take a dog from a rescue service, you will offer them the opportunity to live a better life as they have been treated cruelly or abandoned.

It would be great for them to live in a house full of affection and love.

CHAPTER 3: Prepare your home to welcome your Aussie

3.1 Prepare to welcome your puppy in the best possible way

Before your puppy arrives, you can prepare your home to avoid many disasters and protect all the precious and fragile objects you own.

After extensive research to find the right dog breed, you have chosen an Australian Shepherd. If you have carefully considered the possible options and have decided on the best solution for you, now all you have to do is prepare your home for your furry friend's arrival.

You need to be ready to prevent your Aussie's first day at home from being a huge disaster.

So, you need to make sure your home is tidy and dog-proof.

Remember that the Australian Shepherd is a fast and intelligent dog, so there is a lot of work to be done, and it needs to be done before your puppy gets home. So trust what I'm telling you, and don't waste time.

Dog-proofing your home means securing your belongings and objects, saving money, and avoiding stress. It may seem like a nuisance, but it is necessary for your and your puppy's peace of mind.

While the curiosity is usually cats, the Australian Shepherd is a large, curious dog that crawls all over the place looking for something fragile and chewable that you own.

3.2 The most dangerous areas of the house

Your Australian Shepherd will have a hard time resisting food that he has a much broader view of than you do.

For example, he will be very attracted to the garbage where he could find a nice piece of meat; therefore, you must keep the garbage out of sight, in a large closet, or under the sink.

If you can't hide the trash, you will find the kitchen dirty and littered with food scraps, or, at worst, your puppy could choke to death from something he pulled out of the trash bag.

Another aspect to think about is the electrical cables. When you have a baby in the house, you will have to take them out; here, you must consider your puppy as a child.

Keep the electrical cords tied to the baseboards and apply a scent to them to keep dogs away. In this regard, you could use the hot sauce for your tasty burgers or buy a specific spray at the pet store.

Also, store any extension cords and cables not used in a drawer or closet.

Keep the holiday decorations up as high as possible when the holiday season approaches. Otherwise, your Aussie will tear them off immediately. The decorations usually used in homes look a lot like toys for dogs. Also, avoid poisonous plants like poinsettias.

The main risks your puppy can run are those that can endanger a child: oil lamps, lighted candles, poisonous plants, and medications must be kept out of your dog's reach.

3.3 Arrival of the puppy at home

When bringing your puppy home, you need to keep a few important things in mind. The first is that you are a stranger. The second is that the little Aussie probably never walked away from his mother and siblings or that he never got into a car.

For this reason, you will need to make the journey to your home as less stressful as possible for your puppy so that he can cross the door happy and relaxed.

Once he arrives at the kennel, he spends some time with your puppy, his mother, and his littermates. Ask the breeder for anything you need by placing yourself towards him in an available and polite way.

Building a good relationship with your Australian Shepherd's breeder is essential because it will be useful throughout the puppy's life.

Before letting him leave his kennel, let your puppy go alone to the car and place him in a comfortable and soft place or let him snuggle in the arms of your family member. If he cries or barks on the way, don't worry! This is normal behavior that needs to be handled calmly and patiently.

Your behavior will let him know that you are there to help him. You must use a calm and even tone and not scream or use a harsh attitude toward him; your goal is to show him that you care about his health.

If, during the journey, your puppy has to poop or pee, take him to an area not used by other dogs, and be sure to clean him thoroughly afterward. Your puppy, as he is not yet vaccinated, must avoid exposure to the feces or pee of other dogs that may contain parasites or worms.

As soon as you get home, take your puppy to the potty for him to smell and relieve himself. After he has relieved himself, enter the house and take him to a quiet room, allowing him to discover the surrounding environment. At this point, follow your puppy's signals: if he wants to play or run, let him do it; if he wants to sleep, let him rest. Later, you could introduce your Aussie to other family members, establishing calm and gradual interactions.

In the first few days in his new home, your Australian Shepherd will sleep a lot. This is normal because he is a young puppy.

Over time, however, the time he sleeps will decrease, gaining confidence in his space and abilities.

3.3.1 Other valuable tips and tricks

Allow your puppy to find the level of comfort he needs and make his own decisions in peace. Never force him to do anything against his will. This important socialization process involves bringing your puppy closer to other animals or human beings.

From the first day he arrives at the house, take him for walks and keep him trained with exercises and physical activity.

To make this phase easier, you could take steps before withdrawing your puppy from the breeder. You could send him a blanket a few days earlier and have it rub on your Aussie's littermates and mother.

If you can't do this, bring the blanket with you when you get it so your puppy can start getting used to your scent and associate it with a feeling of security and familiarity.

As for protecting your home, carry out a training program at home and make them respect the rules you impose on them. Your Aussie will learn to use the potty and not climb on the furniture or the sofa through training.

Your puppy must remain in a limited area of the house and will slowly go out to discover the other places as soon as he becomes more confident and as soon as he gains full confidence in himself. To best introduce your puppy to his new home, you must be calm and create rules and schedules that he must abide by.

3.3.2 Tools to have at home

Here are the tools you must have at home before your puppy arrives.

- soft towel or blanket;
- cleaning products;
- collar (make sure it is tight);
- crate;
- neutralizer of pet odors;
- paper towels;
- plastic bags;
- newspapers.

3.4 How to introduce your Australian Shepherd to other family members

After bringing your Aussie indoors, you will need to introduce him to family members.

Even if your first instinct would be to run and introduce him to everyone immediately, your Aussie could get scared and be in a state of confusion caused by excessive attention in no time.

Many people could hide and get scared if a puppy is overwhelmed.

For these reasons, it would be best to introduce your puppy to the rest of the family as calmly as possible and give him time to get used to his new home and many new people.

The first thing you need to do when you bring your puppy home is to let him sleep in a quiet room where there is no one.

Then, when some adjustment time has passed, let him meet family members, one at a time and with utmost peace of mind.

If you also have other pets, wait at least a few days. You don't have to rush but must introduce your new friend correctly to prevent future socialization problems.

3.5 Introduce children

Your youngest children should be introduced to your Australian Shepherd one at a time and not altogether simultaneously.

This way, you can minimize the emotion that the puppy will suffer. On the other hand, older children can also be presented all together.

Have your child enter the room and sit on the floor. You don't have to yell at the Australian Shepherd puppy, and you don't have to put it on your baby's lap; you have to give treats in the hands of your child, who in turn will give them to the puppy to feed him.

Ensure the baby does not scream so the puppy does not get scared. Remember that Australian Shepherds love children, gravitating around them right away. When the puppy meets the baby, allow him to caress him calmly and carefully.

Start with short meetings and gradually increase their duration. Especially during the first busy days, the interactions between the puppy and the children are calm and serene.

When your Australian Shepherd gets used to the sounds and screams of babies, you can increase the moments of play between them.

Children must have rules regarding how to treat and play with the puppy.

Here are the most important rules to teach your children:

- do not keep the puppy if he wants to go away;
- gently caress the puppy;
- be calm with the puppy;
- do not pull the tail and ears;
- do not hit or pinch it with force;
- do not suddenly run away from the puppy;
- do not take away his toys or food;
- use toys only to play with the puppy.

Most puppies do not respect children the same way humans do. Babies can command the puppy with the same authority as they grow up and age.

An adult should always be present when children play with puppies to observe what is happening and avoid dangerous situations.

As children grow up, the dog will respect them more and can even play alone without adult supervision. It is essential to involve the children in training and socializing the Australian Shepherd as he will benefit the puppy, you, and the children.

3.6 Introduce other animals in the house

Other home pets should be introduced gradually to your Australian Shepherd puppy. Pets already in the home may have behavioral problems with a newly arrived puppy and may be jealous of their territory.

You can prevent these problems by ensuring short meetings between them and not forcing relationships; the animals in your home will create a new hierarchy.

There are specific rules to follow when introducing new animals to a home where there already are. We will analyze them in the following pages.

3.6.1 Be patient

Patience is an essential skill to have with your pets. It may happen that they don't accept your Australian Shepherd puppy right away, so you don't have to fret. It may take up to eight months or more for your puppy to be accepted and loved by pets.

3.6.2 How to manage the meeting with cats

Even if you can easily manage the first encounters between your puppy and a dog, you may not be able to control the meeting with a cat.

Puppies often feel curiosity towards cats, perhaps a little too much, and will try to chase them to play with them; when this happens, the cat reacts by running away quickly.

3.6.3 Your puppy must remain confined

One of the first rules is to keep your puppy confined to his new home for the first few days. After that, place your Australian Shepherd in a quiet room, ensuring your current pet feels safe too.

When you get the puppy out of his room, take the current pet elsewhere unless you want to introduce him.

3.6.4 Convey positivity to your current pet

When introducing the Australian Shepherd puppy to the current pet, always give the pet lots of affection.

Also, praise it for kind greetings and give it many treats. If you behave this way, your current pet will positively face the meeting with the new Australian Shepherd puppy.

3.6.5 Make him smell the door or the crate

You should allow your current pet to smell the crate or door the puppy is in. This behavior will help your pet get to know the puppy through a safety barrier. However, don't let it be intrusive, and if your puppy starts crying and getting stressed, stop this behavior immediately.

3.6.6 Create a hierarchy between the pet and the new puppy

You must create a pecking order between the pet already in the house and the Australian Shepherd puppy. This means your pet will have more rights than the puppy and must be fed first; you should greet him when you get home and always allow him to enter or exit first.

3.6.7 Arrange the meeting under the best conditions

Plan meetings between your current pet and the Australian Shepherd puppy in advance. The last thing you need to do is bring a new puppy into the house and let your current pet take over.

Instead, wait until the current pet is calm, and then introduce it to the puppy. Doing so will make possible a positive experience for the new Australian Shepherd and the pet already in the house.

CHAPTER 4: Training your Australian Shepherd

4.1 House training

Before teaching your dog not to enter the house, you must learn to watch and protect your Australian Shepherd as an owner. A puppy must go to the bathroom often, and some accidents may happen because the owner is not carefully observing his dog.

The first rule of home training is to watch your puppy. Next, the puppy will give signals, such as crouching, sniffing around, going to the door, and more. These gestures will mean that your Australian Shepherd must go to the bathroom.

For this reason, if you follow the rules for home training, you will find that your Aussie will learn to train at home in no time.

4.1.1 How to tell when your puppy needs to go to the bathroom

An essential rule of thumb is understanding when your Aussie needs to go to the bathroom.

A puppy dog needs to go to the bathroom:

- about twenty minutes after having eaten or drunk;
- after he has played;
- every 3 hours when awake;
- when he first wakes up.

Follow these rules and take your puppy out of the house to go to the bathroom after each event. Then, you will be able to avoid almost all the accidents that could occur.

4.1.2 Don't scold him

Don't scold your puppy for crouching down to pee or poop - you could frighten him terribly! You won't get anything positive out of scolding a puppy who pees or poops in the house, but you will only realize that your Aussie will be afraid of you.

4.1.3 Praise him continuously

Always praise your dog. When he crouches outside and starts doing business tell him he is a good dog and pet him.

Also, tell him "Do your business" so he'll know it's not the time to play or sniff and go to the bathroom; even if he doesn't defecate right away, he'll associate that phrase with having to pee or poop.

4.1.4 You must be persistent

Repeat this process until he goes to the bathroom on her own. You are training him to go to his crate to prevent him from immediately entering the house and going to the bathroom. After he's out and gone, reward him with treats, and don't pack him too much.

4.2 Potty training

As soon as you let your Australian into your home, you must start home training immediately.

If you wait any longer, he may misbehave or get stuck in bad habits. You have to potty train your Australian Shepherd when he is of the right age and timing, that is, when he is still a puppy; when he becomes an adult, training him will be more complicated and tiring.

Make him understand immediately that the herd lives in your house and that this is his private kingdom. Carry him around, showing him his new environment and his new home.

The main problem with puppies is that they pee and poop every hour and all day. Compared to adult dogs, you will need to give your puppy breaks to pee and poop, and you will need to make him understand that he has to use the jar.

Leave him out every hour and take him to a specific spot in your home so he can take care of his business; if he behaves well and does his business outside, praise and reward him.

You need to make him understand that peeing and pooping outside is good behavior.

A dog often likes to enter the house to mark his territory, especially if the dog has been neutered in old age or is not even neutered.

This can become a problem if there are other dogs in the house, as they see their territory in danger; for example, they will defend the furniture in the house not only so as not to let it ruin but because they claim that furniture is their property.

You could use a hormone spray to keep your dogs from peeing or pooping on furniture.

Reproaching your dog for doing his home business is not effective; you have to teach him commands like "**no**" or "**go out**" as he tries to lift his leg into your new chair. Whenever your puppy tries to mark its territory inside the house, take it to where you have decided it can do business with him.

Decide on a place for your dog to go to the bathroom and take him there as often as you think he should go to the bathroom. You have to say the command "**potty**," and if he pees or poops in the designated place, praise and reward him. You could also use a clicker.

Organize a specific schedule and take it out in its place. When it is a puppy, this will be thirty to sixty minutes; when he is over five months old, roughly every five hours would be fine, while when he is an adult, you can even exceed five hours.

Train him to let you know whenever he needs to go out because not all dogs complain when he gets away from the door. Grab a bell, attach it to your door, and sprinkle it with peanut butter or cheese; whenever he licks and rings, take him out in his potty.

In this way, he will associate the sound of the bell with the exit, and when he has to do his business, he will ring the bell.

4.3 Crate training for the Australian Shepherd

Crate training for your Aussie is a very important moment in his life. You should purchase a nice bed for your Australian Shepherd and train him to use it correctly. With the crate, your puppy will remain calm and can exercise peacefully.

Dogs love a den of their own. They love to hide and crouch in their territory. A crate is a comfortable place and a relaxing hiding place for your dog. Although your home is an excellent place for your puppy to roam, a crate represents the specific space where he can find refuge.

The crate should be a place for your puppy to relax; for this reason, never use the cage as a place of punishment. If you put him in a cage to punish him, he will create a negative association with the cage and be afraid of it. Consequently, he will look for another place to hide, for example, behind the sofa and a piece of furniture, to satisfy his need for daily retreat.

Your dog can be trained at any age and when you pick him up for the first time, give him a few days to understand his new spaces and explore the home. Then, to get him used to his new environment, introduce him to his cage.

Get him into the cage, and if he stays there, praise and rewards him. Then, close the door with the key and leave it there for at least one hour at a time. Be careful never to leave him there for more than three hours without a potty to do his business. To make him feel familiar, put toys or treats in the crate.

Once your Australian Shepherd has become familiar with his new crate, you can leave him inside even if you go outside the house. Once he's fully trained, he leaves the chest door unlocked. Playing inside the box could calm any potential separation anxiety he might have when you're not around.

However, don't leave him in the crate for too long. Please do not turn the crate into a place to serve his punishments. If this happens, he will no longer appreciate the playpen, completely upset his natural habits.

When you are not home, he will get frustrated and start gnawing, biting, howling, crying, barking, scratching, and other negative behaviors.

Any dog needs a peaceful and safe place to call "**home**" and where he can relax. Your home is a nice place to roam, but it doesn't represent the den dogs want.

It is the crate that satisfies a dog's desire for a den as well as offers comfort and protection.

All puppies should learn to have fun and relax in their crate; therefore, the crate should never be used as a punishment.

Before getting your Australian Shepherd into the crate, train them for a couple of days to adapt to their new surroundings. Next, train him in the cage. Your dog's love for his kennel is important and allows you to take care of him forever.

Gradually limit the time your puppy stays in the cage to about one hour for each session. Never leave your Aussie in a crate for more than four hours without ever letting him out.

When your dog grows up and won't chew on everything he sees, you can leave the crate door open so he can run around the house freely.

4.4 Leave the Australian Shepherd alone

Don't get too much trouble when you go out, and don't have overreactions that could cause separation anxiety from your boss. This attitude is harmful to our four-legged friends.

Before you go out, ensure your dog stays in a place with a comfortable temperature, has cool water, and has plenty of toys to spend time with. Let the puppy let off steam and tire before you leave.

When you leave, greet him with a positive tone of voice and a simple phrase, such as **"Hello, I'll be back soon**." If you welcome him dramatically, you could create a situation of fear and worry, increasing your puppy's anxiety level, resulting in many negative behaviors.

When you return, behave similarly. Don't look your puppy in the eye immediately, and don't run to him like it's been months since you last saw him.

If your absence has lasted more than an hour, pick him up and say hello, followed by a short break. After he's done pissing him off, put him back in his restricted area and go back to doing what you were doing.

CHAPTER 5: Socialization with people and other animals

5.1 The importance of socializing your Australian shepherd

It is essential to socialize the Australian Shepherd puppy when he is still at an early age because if he is well socialized, he will not be aggressive towards people or other animals.

Through this training, he will understand that different people and animals exist and that they are not a threat or danger to his territory. Without adequate socialization, any dog would be convinced that it is the only one in the world to exist and that no other living being has the authorization to enter.

Furthermore, an unsocialized dog would get angry whenever another person or animal showed up.

So, as soon as your Aussie enters the house, you need to socialize with him, getting him used to tolerating other people and animals in his territory.

5.1.2 The basics of socialization

After only three weeks of birth, your puppy begins the socialization process. Up to four months after birth, he socializes with his siblings and his mother, learning to play and share spaces with them.

To achieve good socialization, expose your puppy to different environments. Take it for a walk, to the park, to the sea or the lake; take it to places where other dogs and humans are playing, walking, or exercising. Show him different landscapes and environments so he can get used to the variety of the world around him.

He must realize that trains, cars, and planes make noises.

Take him to all the rooms in your home, put him on the stairs, or walk him down the hallway, always ensuring he is tied with a leash.

This process will teach him to be curious and not fear new things. A dog that adapts to all environments is well-mannered and good. Let your friends play with your Australian Shepherd puppy, so he gets used to them and learns to love other people. You don't have to make him overly fond of you; doing so would fear and would distrust other people.

Play with him often, so you bond closely. Teach him what is right and unsuitable when he relates to other people. Show him that you are a good teacher and deserve his trust, and let him know that you love him and have fun and peaceful moments with him.

He always finds new stimulating physical and mental activities to keep him active and engaged.

You need to give your Aussie some time to be alone, so you can learn not to be anxious when you can't be with him. Let him play outside with other dogs but not with you, or leave him alone in his case for at least two hours a day to sleep.

Discipline is essential to prevent and avoid bad habits from the very beginning. Tell him "**No**" if he messes around the house, if he bites you while you are playing, or if he still doesn't understand how to use the potty.

Your Australian Shepherd puppy doesn't have to get away with it but needs to realize that there are rules to abide by. If you teach him this, he will understand what is allowed and not, and he will become a kinder and more obedient dog.

Socialize your Australian Shepherd puppy when he is six weeks old. The socialization period is essential for a dog's growth and usually ranges from **8-16 weeks**.

In this phase, the puppies must interact and become familiar with other humans and animals correctly and effectively.

Be aware of your puppy's reactions. If you see that he reacts well, offer him more opportunities to socialize, but if he does not respond adequately, understand the problem and calm him down.

This learning phase needs to be handled well as it is the foundation for your puppy's healthy growth.

5.1.3 The perfect greeting

Would you like your puppy to greet someone arriving at your home, but at the same time, would you also want him to stay still?

Would you like to avoid that awkward moment when your dog barks at your visitor? To avoid this, call him to get him to stop barking.

Ask your friend who comes into the house to do anything that makes the dog bark inappropriately: knock on the door, open the door, walk past the house.

Your Australian Shepherd puppy should be on a leash, ready for training. When your friend does anything that makes your puppy bark, command him to come in in a calm, confident voice.

At this point, the puppy will come towards you, and you will have to give him a treat, showing him first for a few moments.

After some training, your puppy will learn. But, of course, it will never wholly stop barking and will continue to spot you in the presence of a stranger at home; the difference is that it will know how to stop when you command it.

CHAPTER 6: Physical and mental exercises for your Australian Shepherd

6.1 Physical activity

The Australian Shepherd as a breed requires a very high amount of exercise, including **3-4 walks on a leash daily**. Walks with your puppy must be done correctly, without pulling; this exercise will create a strong bond between you and your dog both physically and mentally.

You need to allow time for your dog to exercise regularly every day. If this doesn't happen, your Australian Shepherd will be overweight, stressed, unhappy, and unhealthy. In addition, it could also develop severe health and behavioral problems.

The health of your Australian Shepherd depends so much on the physical exercise he can do. Your dog needs to be taken outside to run, play or walk.

Remember, this breed is bred for hard work and always needs what it does to be physically and mentally engaged. Your Aussie will be bored to death if he stays locked up at home for long. And a bored and tired Aussie will soon become a destructive dog.

The Australian Shepherd needs exercise. Otherwise, he may get angry and become unmanageable.

So have him take three or four daily walks for about thirty minutes each. You may also be exercising with them; Australian Shepherds are excellent jogging and running companions and are suitable for long walks.

Your dog must spend some free time off the leash because it is perfect for his health. Leave him off the leash in a safe area or your yard so he can run freely, chase prey, herd local squirrels or rabbits, and chase balls. All of this will make your Australian Shepherd very happy.

6.1.1 The minimum amount of daily exercise

Your Aussie should be taken out at least three times a day for at least one hour for each walk. He must walk disciplined on a leash, without pulling and obeying your commands.

After he is properly leashed trained and he learns to listen to basic commands, your Australian Shepherd will need a hefty reward; take him to a fenced dog park where he can run, socialize, and play with other dogs with a Frisbee or a ball.

6.1.2 Carry out a correct workout

You are responsible for the physical activity and games your dog plays. If you are not aware of what you are teaching him, your Australian Shepherd may be engaging in misbehavior.

He may never forget this mistake, and correcting it may take a long time.

For example, if your dog barks and you immediately throw him the desired object, such as the ball or the Frisbee, you will teach him that to get what he wants, he must swear or bark.

This is precisely what you have to avoid doing.

6.2 Mental exercises for your Australian Shepherd

The Australian Shepherd is very dedicated to working and takes what is asked of him seriously. But unfortunately, he has an instinct that will lead him to round up children and other pets in the house. If this behavior becomes a problem, you will need to give him some training.

Australian Shepherds are easy to train, being highly intelligent dogs. They excel in running and agility in dog sports, and many Australian Shepherd owners win many awards thanks to their dogs.

You must spend some time keeping your Aussie busy through lots of mental exercises. Below you will find the description of the 3 fundamental mental exercises to make him perform.

6.2.1 Mental exercise of the frozen morsel

The first exercise is to fill a bowl with beef or chicken broth and a dog morsel. Next, return the bowl to the freezer and, once frozen, take it out and turn it upside down in the sink pouring hot water over it for a few seconds.

Take the bowl out into the garden and turn it upside down, tapping lightly until the frozen morsel comes off and falls to the ground. The puppy will take time to understand the situation and grab the frozen treat in the center.

6.2.2 Mental exercise of playing hide and seek

The second mental exercise is to play hide and seek. First, you must teach your Australian Shepherd the "sit down" command; this game can be fascinating once that is done. Next, have your dog sit down and stay next to him for a few moments. Then, leave the area and hide well. After you find a hiding place, he calls the dog and asks him to come and see you. To make the game even more fun and educational, place a treat in your hand and reward it when your puppy finds you.

6.2.3 Mental exercise of taking him for a walk

The third exercise is to walk the dog. If you have to shop or run errands, bring your Australian Shepherd with you.

Your puppy will be able to see exciting things and will also have something to do.

At the same time, you can spend more time with him. Keep your car windows open to circulate the air if it's not cold.

But be careful not to open them so much that your Aussie pops out.

CHAPTER 7: How to Train Your Aussie

Dogs like training because they appreciate the human interaction and enjoy pleasing their owners.

With training, in addition to strengthening the bond with your dog, you will be able to show other dog owners the exercises they will be able to perform.

7.1 The essential elements of training

The five most important aspects of training any dog are these:

- positive reinforcement;
- patience;
- confidence;
- consistency;
- repetition.

Your dog must be well socialized and accustomed to your presence and management. Training your dog must take place sometime after you bought it. This is because he will not trust you yet and may be stressed or scared of the training process.

Puppies are more adaptable to training and are quick to understand new tricks.

However, puppies also have less attention span, which could complicate the training process. Adult dogs are less physically willing to train but have a higher attention span.

7.2 The prerequisites for successful training

Even before you train your dog, you need to understand how he spends his time and what food he loves so that you can adequately reward him when he does your bidding.

You will need to find a couple of healthy treats to reward your puppy and, at the same time, keep him healthy even during the training phase.

In this regard, it is advisable to reward your Australian Shepherd puppy with a morsel of the liver, a piece of chicken, or a raw carrot.

If you know your puppy's preferences well, you can work without difficulty, indulging his natural inclinations and praising your desired behaviors with a prize.

7.3 Attention and focus

Just one of the most important aspects of training a dog is teaching him attention and focus towards you. Shout out your puppy's name and reward him for paying attention if he gives it to you.

Repeat this training several times and make sure the Australian Shepherd has an adequate level of attention when you call him.

Your puppy's behavior needs to be modeled through positive reinforcement.

Concentrate fully on this work out and make eye contact until you convince him.

7.4 The technique of positive reinforcement instead of punishment

Never punish your Australian Shepherd if he doesn't do what you want. Instead, you must teach him not to engage in destructive behavior by shortening the play time or picking up a toy. Teach what you want with a good reward in exchange for his obedience.

Punishing the puppy may have adverse effects on your relationship. This way, he will be afraid of you and will not become your trusted and obedient friend.

Instead, he'll be motivated to make you happy and see you as his leader with positive reinforcement. He will try to please you because he knows you will reward him with a delicious treat.

First, you need to offer rewards for good behavior. This is the basis of training your Australian Shepherd puppy. Use a clicker, a prize, and tons of praise to train your Aussie.

Then, after learning their preferences well, teach them to associate obedience to you with obtaining a reward.

The reward must mean a lot to him so that he has more power over him. If your dog likes to go to a park near your home, you may want to reward his correct behavior by saying the phrase **"let's go to the park near home**."

Thus, he will quickly learn the phrase's meaning and associate the reward with what he is ordered to do. The most powerful motivators are the rewards and treats.

Always show the love you feel towards your Australian Shepherd. Praise him just because he's lying next to you or because he's your friend. Any dog loves to feel helpful to you.

If you show love and affection to your Australian Shepherd, you will create a strong bond that will last a lifetime.

Punishment teaches dogs nothing. Indeed, the sentence will confuse your puppy, scare him and stress him a lot; they are all terrible mental states for your dog. A dog usually destroys a piece of furniture or a sofa because he is taking out his anger at you.

Instead, he needs to understand what he did wrong. When your Australian Shepherd puppy is destroying something, clap your hands and call him by name to get his attention. Once you get his attention, focus on letting him know where he went wrong.

7.5 Consistency as a fundamental element

Another critical element in training your Aussie is consistency. You must always anticipate a consequence for everything your dog does.

Bad behavior must never be tolerated or forgiven, while good behavior always pays off. In addition, you must always be consistent with your commands; therefore, choose a command that works well and always use it.

If you change the controls, you will confuse your Aussie because he won't know what you want. Finally, having a coherent training program is ideal for the dog's well-being and peace of mind.

If you train him regularly, you will get better results. Also, feed him, clean him, and play with him at regular and consistent times. The dog will get used to the schedules and always know what to expect.

This process will help your Australian Shepherd puppy learn more easily and become a good dog.

CHAPTER 8: The basic commands to make your Aussie obey

8.1 "Sit!"

One of the first commands your Australian will need to learn is how to sit. To be able to teach him this command, you must proceed as follows.

1) Have your Australian Shepherd stand in front of you.

2) Take a treat, place it in your right hand and let him smell it, being careful not to drop it.

3) Say the phrase "**sit!**" Once.

4) Put the tidbit over his head slowly and see if his muzzle follows him and his butt drops. When his butt lands on the ground, use the click to let him know he's right.

5) You have to be patient as it may take a long time to get the behavior you want from your Australian Shepherd. You must never force your Aussie to do something he doesn't want to do; this attitude will activate his reflex of opposition, interrupting any learning he has had up to that point. If you see that it doesn't work, take a relaxing break and resume training later.

6) Don't correct or punish your puppy if he misbehaves. This will lead to serious behavioral problems and make him less eager to learn new things.

8.2 "Stay!"

"**Stay**!" is another basic command you must teach your puppy. This signal is very important for your Aussie's education and can be used with other signals. To teach him this signal, do the following.

1) Ask your puppy to sit up.

2) Cover his nose with your hand and say the word "**stay!**".

3) Spend five seconds, click and reward him with a treat if he does.

4) Gradually increase the duration of the workout, waiting a few more seconds between the click and the treatment.

If your Australian Shepherd puppy can complete the training several times, he begins to move away gradually after giving him the signal with the click.

Pet him and reward him if your Aussie stands still. Then, repeat the training twice daily and increase the distance between you and him.

If he moves, do not punish or scold him but repeat the exercise on a less complicated level. Reward him if he does it correctly. Remember that calmness and patience will pay off any effort you make.

8.3 "Down!"

With this command, you can teach your Australian Shepherd puppy to lie down. You should teach this signal after your puppy has learned to sit because it is often an action. To prepare the "**down!**" you must proceed with the following steps.

1) Ask your puppy to sit in front of you.

2) Take a treat, put it in your right hand, and let him smell it, avoiding reaching it. Next, move the tidbit from nose to toe; after a few tries, it should slowly lie down. Repeat the training with persistence and patience if your dog does not behave as you want.

3) The moment he rests his front elbows on the ground, click and reward him with a treat. Repeat the exercise several times.

4) When your Aussie does this exercise correctly, shout the word "**down**" as you click. Then, praise your puppy, pet him and reward him with a treat.

5) After several exercises, he starts shouting the word "**down**" before his elbows touch the floor. He continues to click when his elbows touch the ground, and when the training becomes more intense, he always pronounces the signal earlier.

It could take several weeks of training for your Australian Shepherd to learn this command. Never use force and never punish your pup for keeping him in position.

8.4 "Come!"

This is one of the most complicated basic commands to teach your Australian Shepherd puppy. During this training, you will need more confidence in your dog. So first, when you first train him, keep him on a leash.

Never use punishment when doing this exercise. You must never punish your Australian Shepherd puppy if he misbehaves. If you do this, he will learn that the command "come!" has a negative meaning and will never come to you.

Instead, use this command to make bonding with your dog wonderful. Praise and give him many treats; this way, he will come to you. Show yourself as interesting and exciting, and you will see that he will run to you.

You can do this training in two ways: the first is when you sit him down and stay close to him to call him. Your puppy will almost always come to you if something is interesting to look at or take. This is a targeted way to reach your dog, but it is not the only one.

The second way to do this exercise is when he is distracted and can also be taught on a leash.

To teach both ways to execute the "**how**" command, you must proceed as follows.

1) Put a leash around your dog and let him sit or search for food in front of your eyes. Use a leash of at least 50 feet so you can call him to come to you at different distances.

2) If he is sitting, move away from him and call him with the "**come**" signal. If he starts moving, wait for your Aussie to get distracted.

3) Call him with the "**how**" signal and then encourage him to come to you by flapping his legs so he will get excited and run to you. Then, give him a gift without repeating the signal.

4) Go in the opposite direction even though this may tighten the leash. Once your Australian Shepherd approaches you, praise him and give him treats and treats.

5) As soon as your puppy reaches you, guide him to sit down with a treat without giving the signal.

6) Praise your Aussie, pet him and reward him with a treat.

7) Insist on this workout for several days. After your Australian Shepherd puppy becomes adept and comes to you a few feet away, gradually increase the distance. The goal is to practice until he is more than 100 feet away from you and keeps coming when you call him, even if he is on a leash.

8.5 "Drop it!"

This command can save your Australian Shepherd's life because he will teach him to drop anything you want. It is a simple command to learn, but it is still necessary that your puppy has something to take and that he is prepared to carry out the exercise. The following steps are required to train your Aussie with the "**drop it**" command.

1) Have your puppy grab something with his mouth; to encourage him, you could play with him.

2) When he puts something in his mouth, take it with one hand and put a morsel in the other. Now use the "drop it" command.

3) Bring the treat close to his nose so he can smell it.

4) If he drops the object, praise and rewards him with the treat.

5) If he does not drop the object, move the morsel in his mouth, and you will see that it will fall.

6) As soon as he drops the object, praise and rewards him.

8.6 "Leave it!"

This signal is also significant because it could save your dog's life. Teaching your puppy to let things sit will prevent them from picking up dangerous items and eating them on a walk. Practice gradually to teach him this command. Leave things in your hands first, and then leave something on the ground.

1) Take a treat, put it in your hand, and close your fist.

2) Hold your hand in front of your dog's muzzle and use the "**leave it**" command.

3) Make him smell the tidbit and try to take it. If he gets it, ignore it.

4) When he stops, even for a few moments, praise your puppy and give him a treat with the other hand. But don't use the hand you told him to go away with. Repeat this exercise several times.

5) Over time, as your puppy improves, the difficulty of the exercise increases. First, take the treat and place it on your open hand, then put it under your cupped hand, and then place it on the ground without covering it. When your Australian Shepherd puppy doesn't touch the treat, always reward him.

CHAPTER 9: Changing Your Australian Shepherd's Unwanted Behaviours

9.1 Jumping on people

Australian Shepherds usually jump on the people they love. This is an affectionate form of greeting, particularly towards you. They want to overwhelm you with their love for you.

They want to be caressed because they are happy that you are back. Jumping is their way of getting your attention. While all of this can be enjoyable when your dog is a puppy, it can become annoying as it grows and maybe stout in size.

It could disturb friends who visit you or ruin dinners with your relatives, making their presence unpleasant.

In addition, a large dog like the Australian Shepherd can get your clothes or pants dirty; it can scratch your legs and cause you to slip or drop your groceries if unbalanced on its hind legs.

These are all events that can happen. For this reason, you must teach him early on that jumping on people is not correct and polite behavior.

When your dog jumps on you, yell "**no!**". You go out of the room and return after a few minutes. Repeat this exercise several times; he will understand that you don't like him jumping on you.

Tell him "**No!**" even when jumping on other people; when the puppy wants to greet friends and family improperly, invite them to leave the room.

Reward your Australian Shepherd with lots of love when he stops jumping on you and your friends or family. Drop to his height to reward him and show him that he doesn't need to hop on you to get your attention; you will always give it to him at his level when he is ready.

If your Aussie doesn't stop jumping on people despite your best efforts to train them, practice for longer. He continues the training even if he engages in other wrong behaviors, such as, for example, the hindrance in moving his paws.

When he rocks, jumps, or misbehaves, you must pull him away from the room and tie him up for a few minutes.

This method should only be used if you fail otherwise. Your Australian Shepherd, if well trained, will immediately obey your every command.

9.2 Chewing properly

Chewing is a natural behavior that any dog exhibits. The brilliant smile every day gives you depends on proper chewing with its long and sharp teeth.

In addition, chewing helps the dog maintain healthy teeth, and teething puppies are particularly prone to chewing whatever they find because they are teething.

You need to give your Australian Shepherd safe chew toys and bones to keep his mouth and mind busy when he gets bored.

If you catch your Australian Shepherd chewing on your new shoes, take them off immediately and tell him he doesn't have to. Get a bone or a toy and say, "**good boy**." If he doesn't want to leave your shoes, he uses a deterrent spray to make them unpalatable. He won't want to chew them even for a second if they taste awful.

9.3 Digging

Some dog breeds dig because they are bred specifically to search for prey. Other species dig into building a cool den where they can lie down and rest; other races still do it because they are bored. Dogs are fascinated by sand and soft dirt and fondly for breaking things.

You could teach your Australian Shepherd to dig in certain places so that he does not dig anywhere. Instead, create a specific dig spot and lets him have fun. To make the game even better, bury bones or toys and let him dig for them. Every dog love to do this activity.

If your Australian Shepherd digs in places where he is not allowed, say "No" and fill the hole he dug with bottle caps, cans, and coins and see how your dog reacts.

Then, when he starts digging, hit the objects you buried so that he gets scared; he will therefore create an association between digging and the metallic sound of the things you hit, thus stopping digging at that point.

9.4 Barking

To teach your Australian Shepherd not to bark, use the prevention tool. The goal is not to make your dog's soft furry head bark when he sees you and when he gets scared or curious.

After all, someone knocks on the door, and he hears a loud noise at that moment. When he barks out of boredom or frustration, switch his attention to another exciting activity. Barking for no proper reason is annoying to you and your neighbors, which is why it should be avoided.

Dogs bark by nature. Barking is your dog's response to so many things. He could warn you of imminent danger; he could warn other dogs or animals to get away; he may bark to greet you, express his happiness at seeing you, or defend his territory. He may also be bored, so barking would be a way to distract himself.

For example, my awesome Aussie barks when I sleep too much and wants to wake me up to play together. Dogs usually do brilliant things when they want to achieve something.

However, when the problematic behavior is barking for no reason, it is not difficult to correct it.

9.5 Chasing

Your Aussie loves to chase its prey. And he loves even more to chase objects he sees as his prey.

This may be an annoying behavior, however. To teach your Aussie Shepherd not to pursue any prey, you can use the word "**look at me**" to get him to shift his attention to you and not to the game he wants to chase.

You could also use a clicker and a treat to teach him not to hunt animals; when he wants to pursue them, give him the command to sit or look at you. Then, take the treat and when he looks at you, click and reward him.

As soon as it understands that it will get a reward if it listens to you, it will soon stop chasing its prey.

With the "**timeout**" method, you can intervene when the dog does not want to listen. Catch it, take it out of the prey it wants to chase and keep it tied up for at least five minutes. Use this method even if it hunts you against your will.

Train your Australian Shepherd to come towards you when you yell his name. Then, when he is in the mood to hunt a person or other animal, he must distract himself by obeying your command to come.

Your Australian Shepherd must be kept on a leash when you are out and about. He remembers that his hunting instinct is strong, and it's difficult to hold back or calm down. In these situations, you will need to protect yourself, your dog, other people, and other animals by keeping him tight on a leash.

If you have other dogs or cats in the house, your **Australian Shepherd** will get used to being friends with them and will see them neither as prey nor as his tasty snack. Socialization and interaction with other animals will teach him to respect them.

9.6 Nipping

From an early age, you must teach your Aussie not to bite your body, your hands, and others. You can practice playing with him while holding a chew toy. You have to make him understand that he can bite the chew toy, not scold him when he does. If he bites your hand, you scream in pain, and he leaves the room.

So, he will get sad because the game is over, and he will understand that he will no longer have to bite you if he wants to play with you.

If he doesn't stop biting despite moving away, you could try moderation to get him to associate the pause with the bite. Shout out the word **"timeout"** the moment he bites, take him to his timeout zone, and tie him up for five minutes ignoring him.

Also, teach your children and family members not to get bitten by your Australian Shepherd. Teach them not to run away as your Australian Shepherd may take this as an invitation to hunt them; instead, it teaches them to hold the position or scream in pain without running away and giggling.

Another important thing is to teach your Australian Shepherd to eat politely. When you feed him, use the command **"polite"** and reward him for chewing the food well. If he wants to bite, remove the food and take it away from him.

You could make your Aussie stop biting by giving him commitments. Biting could be a complex problem to overcome, especially if your Aussie is a puppy and is in the teething phase. Get him lots of toys and bones to chew on to keep his mouth busy. He must understand that he can chew these objects, but he must not chew you, other people, and other animals.

9.7 Running away

Your dog could get into trouble when he runs away if he doesn't get hurt or even die. You must teach your Australian Shepherd not to run away when he sees something that intrigues him or when he is bored.

A good way to dissuade your Australian Shepherd from running away is to spay or neuter him early. Dogs run away because they need to mate. If you don't want to spay or neuter your dog because you want him to have puppies, then you need to keep him inside when he is in heat.

When you go out, always take him on a leash and in a fenced area so he doesn't run away as soon as he sees a mate to mate with. A dog in heat will stop at nothing to mate.

Even looking from the window can be dangerous. If your Australian Shepherd manages to escape but comes home alone, give him a treat.

You have to show him that he is loved because even if he runs away, he still has the desire to go home.

The main goal is to prevent your dog from escaping; this behavior is dangerous for him, other people, and other animals that come across him.

9.8 Aggression

It's never okay if your dog is aggressive. Your dog's aggression could depend on various reasons. The best way to reduce his aggression is to let him know that it must never be directed toward other people and can never be tolerated except in dangerous circumstances.

You need to stay calm first and not be aggressive with him. Show that you are in charge, but not that you are aggressive. You never have to back down, or your Aussie will think you are not the boss.

If something makes your dog aggressive, you must teach him to go to his crate immediately.

Practice ringing the bell or presenting him with a trigger and then have him go to his chest and give him a treat. When you are inside his crate, have him associate the clicker with entering his crate.

Then use the clicker whenever something happens that can make him aggressive and reward him with treats and praise when he enters his crate. The crate is handy when your Australian Shepherd is afraid or angry because it is the only safe place where he can relax.

You could also use the **"timeout"** method when your Australian Shepherd is aggressive towards other people.

In these situations, tell him no and keep him tied up for at least five minutes until he stops growling and barking. He will learn that if he becomes aggressive, he will have to remain alone and away from other people or animals.

With this training, he will stop being aggressive because he will want to stay in the same room as you are.

If your dog's aggression depends on his fear, remove him from what scares him and give him a treat, thus breaking him from this fear. Then, have him expose his fears from a safe distance and reassure him with calm, kind words. You will make him believe that you will always solve all problems and that his fears are unfounded.

Reward him well for staying calm in a situation where he can usually get nervous and aggressive. You need to teach him that the ideal behavior is to be quiet, praise and reward him when he remains calm.

An effective trick with Australian Shepherd puppies is to manage their toys and food as you please.

He must understand from an early age that you can touch his things and that he must not become territorial when you feel what he considers his property.

You will teach him to accept that you take his things and not to be aggressive with you.

CHAPTER 10 Traveling smoothly with your Australian Shepherd

10.1 Local travel with your Aussie

Traveling with an Australian Shepherd in a car can create several problems. Your dog may be barking, moaning, throwing up, or moving around.

For some dogs, the car can generate anxiety with the consequence that even short journeys could become dramatic.

The following pages will describe the most important rules that will allow your Australian Shepherd to feel comfortable on the move, making your journey relaxing and fun.

10.1.1 Be patient and know how to plan

Before introducing your Australian Shepherd into your car, you need to know that a lot of patience is required. You must first let your dog explore your vehicle a long time before his first trip.

If you present the car directly to him on the day of his first trip, he may suffer from anxiety or fear of this new experience. For this reason, you need to plan a series of exercises to introduce your Australian Shepherd to your car.

10.1.2 Use perfume to mark the territory

Even after your Aussie gets used to your car, travel will always bring him a lot of excitement and happiness. Having your dog mark his territory inside your vehicle is extremely important to allow him to have a specific place inside the rear passenger compartment or trunk that he can consider his space.

Your dog will become familiar with his space, thus being able to relax more. You could make his space more comfortable by bringing his favorite toys, pillows, and blankets.

Your Australian Shepherd's favorite items, which are already covered with his scent, will make him feel comfortable with him and help him relax inside the car.

10.1.3 Importance of security

Attention should be paid to the safety of your furry friend during all car journeys. Therefore, you should install a divider between the passenger area and the car's trunk to prevent the dog from causing problems while driving.

You should also use dog carriers and dog-specific safety belts. In addition, different countries, states, and areas may have different rules and regulations regarding the transportation of dogs by car.

Therefore, before leaving, you should inform yourself about the traffic codes of the state or country where you intend to go. You will be safe and avoid incurring unpleasant fines for violating the road rules.

10.2 Going overseas with your Aussie

Most people believe it is challenging to travel abroad with a dog. For this, buy a dog when he decides to start a family. But did you know that dog lovers can safely travel abroad with their four-legged friends? The dog is probably man's best friend. Why should you leave him alone at home? Always carry it with you.

10.2.1 Where to go with your Australian Shepherd

If you go to a place with a very different climate than the one you live in, bring tools with you to facilitate the adaptation to the change in temperature. Bring coats, sweaters, and heavy shoes for your Aussie if you will be traveling to a cold place.

Bring a pair of light shoes, a cooling jacket, and lots of water if you are going to an area with a hot climate; beware of hot ground, which could become dangerous for your furry friend's paws.

You could also fill the cooling jacket with water and make it work, similar to an ice pack. An inexpensive cooling jacket costs around $ 15.

10.2.2 Check the rules for traveling with your dog

Before deciding when to leave, check the transport services, airlines, and border control regulations. You need to know what awaits you during your trip abroad. The rules on the transport of dogs vary from country to country: some countries have stricter rules on the importation of dogs, while others will have more flexible rules.

You can transport your Australian Shepherd on a plane in three different ways:

- take it to the aircraft cabin;
- embark it as luggage;
- board it on another cargo flight.

Major airlines allow pets up to 45 cm in length, 30 cm in width, and 25 cm in height to be taken on board with a maximum weight of 10 kg. However, most regulations will not allow you to leave your dog out of a carrier if you travel in the cabin. The reason is the fear that dogs may run along the aisle for the duration of the journey, thus disturbing other passengers.

10.2.3 The equipment to have for your trip

Here is the equipment you absolutely must have to travel more easily with your dog.

Harness at the waist

With this tool, you can have your hands accessible, and you can leave your dog next to you under control. The waist harness is necessary if you want to hike, allowing you to walk in peace with your dog. You can also use this accessory when you need both hands to carry your suitcase correctly.

Pet passport

Many countries, including all European countries, require a pet passport to transport your dog. The pet passport indicates important data about your dog, such as the latest vaccination for diseases such as rabies. In addition, it has plenty of room for you to update your pet's medical history.

Most veterinarians issue this passport. If your vet does not issue it, you should be told the closest place to get a pet passport.

Most vets will issue pet passports, but if not, I recommend asking the vet to tell you where the closest location is to get a pet passport. Pet passports have plenty of room to update your pet's medical history.

IATA (International Air Transportation Association) pet kennel

It is advisable to buy an **IATA** pet bed because it will save you numerous problems when you board your dog in the trunk of an airplane or keep it with you in the cabin. This kennel is made of sturdy plastic with air holes on all sides and has a metal door that guarantees a secure closure system. In addition, any airline will authorize boarding at an IATA cash desk.

10.2.4 Arrival at destination

You need to have a specific schedule of what to do when you arrive at your destination to minimize stress for you and your puppy. In particular, you must:

- make sure you have booked a hotel that allows pets;
- have established a path with easy access to food and water for your dog;
- check local pet regulations.

Many people carry their pets on a pet-friendly cargo flight. If you decide so too, you must take a plane that lands at the same destination airport as the cargo plane, and you must book accommodation where your dog can await your arrival. Please don't ruin your trip but think of everything you need first.

CHAPTER 11: The Perfect Diet for Your Australian Shepherd

Feeding your Australian Shepherd isn't just about putting dog food in their bowl. You must first understand the proper diet to provide your dog for his physical and mental health. Avoid foods with chemicals and buy quality foods that reduce many health problems.

11.1 Variety of dog food

Before feeding your Australian Shepherd, you should look at the various foods the market offers. Many dog food brands are available in every pet store, so selecting a specific one cannot be easy.

11.1.1 Dry food

The cheapest and most common dog food is dry food. These are flake food, kibble, biscuits, and mixes. It is the most accessible food to store and may be the best choice if your Australian Shepherd is large.

11.1.2 Wet food

Wet food is usually canned and is similar to canned fish. However, it has a very high humidity level and is more caloric and expensive than dry food.

If your dog is huge, wet food is not the best choice due to the high cost per gram and the fact that many cans should be fed daily. However, it could be used to season dog kibble or as an additional meal. You should always check the amount of kibble you provide your Australian Shepherd. Failing this, the dog may gain too much weight.

11.1.3 Semi-moist food

Semi-moist food is commonly stored in a small bag and is shaped like a kibble in gravy. Semi-moist food is also more expensive than dry food and is given to a dog for some special event. It must be mixed with dry food to be eaten as a morsel or condiment.

11.1.4 Homemade raw food

Another variety of food that you could feed your Australian Shepherd is homemade raw food. This food has many benefits for your dog, such as the high quantity and nutrients. You could adapt the raw food to your Aussie's needs or add some fruit and vegetables to it.

Also, dogs tend to use more nutrients with raw food than other types of food, resulting in less litter scattered around the house to collect.

But remember that if raw food is not prepared or stored correctly, your Australian Shepherd could be at risk of bacterial poisoning such as salmonella.

An additional disadvantage of raw food is that if you create the recipes yourself, you could give them meals with severe nutritional deficiencies.

Before you give your Australian Shepherd any of the foods listed, you need to ensure its good quality, chemical-free, and packed with nutrients. Your dog will grow healthy if he eats food with these characteristics.

11.2 When to feed your Australian Shepherd

Your Aussie's nutrition depends on age and how you organize your daily tasks. Generally, your puppy should be fed at least three times a day: once in the morning, once for lunch, and once in the evening.

When your puppy grows up, you can reduce it to twice a day, skipping the meal at lunchtime. The important thing is that you never go down to just once a day. A feed could give your dog stomach problems with serious consequences for his growth.

Start the day by giving your Australian Shepherd breakfast.

Then, while he eats, you prepare yourself so that he will be finished just before you leave for work.

11.3 The amount of food to be administered

The amount of food your dog must eat varies according to age, physical activity, and the type of diet it is taking. A low-quality food should be consumed in larger quantities, while high-quality food can be consumed in smaller quantities.

This is a general rule you must respect for your Australian Shepherd to reach the necessary caloric intake.

To establish proper nutrition, you must consider your dog's age, weight, and energy level. You must know the energy needs at rest, i.e., the number of calories your dog burns while sleeping.

Starting from this data, you will be able to know the exact amount of food and calories that you must give to your dog to meet its energy needs. This operation, although it may seem complex, is effortless.

We can describe it in the following passages:

- weigh your dog;
- multiply its weight by 30;
- add 70.

So, if you have a 24-pound Australian Shepherd:

- divide 24 by 2.2 for a total of 10.9;
- multiply 10.9 by 30 for a total of 327;
- add 70 to 327 for a total of 397 calories per day.

Almost all dog food brands offer pouches with the number of calories divided for each cup or half cup. Your job is only to divide the calories needed by the calories provided.

11.4 Water for your Australian Shepherd

You must offer your four-legged friend water throughout the day. The warmer the season, the more water you will have to give; in the summer months, he will drink more water than in the winter. The water should be cold, but not icy, as it could cause severe digestive problems.

For a young Australian Shepherd who is not fully house trained, you should only offer water at certain times.

Doing this will drastically reduce the number of times your puppy goes to the bathroom. Another rule of thumb, if your dog is young, is to remove the water bowl 2 hours before sleep. This way, the puppy will get through the night without any problems.

If your Australian Shepherd is an adult or trained, you can always leave the water on the floor.

11.5 Sweets to reward your Aussie

On the shelves of any pet store, you will find an endless variety of treats to give your puppy. Unfortunately, some sweets contain only one ingredient, and choosing among many types will not be easy.

CHAPTER 12: Caring for and brushing your Aussie

12.1 The basis for effective brushing

Your Australian Shepherd needs to be brushed thoroughly once a week. Removing loose hair, small objects stuck in its coat, or any mats is necessary. The Australian Shepherd is a curious dog, so don't be surprised if you find small pieces of twig tangled in his fur or the like.

Its coat comprises two layers: the top coat, which is long and silky, and the undercoat, which is very dense and changes according to the seasons. Also, for this reason, it is essential to brush it frequently.

You could buy a grooming table with the money saved if you do not pay for a groomer. This will be especially useful if you play in the fields or go on many hikes in the woods. However, it is not essential, and the important thing is that you find a place where you can clean up all the things you sweep away from his coat.

Initially, use a smoother brush. This type of wide-toothed comb is an excellent tool for breeds with a double coat because it has a stainless-steel rake and curved wire bristles. You have to tackle one section of the hair at a time, moving from the skin to the tips of the hair.

As you go, keep cleaning the fur from the rake and pick up a second brush that can pull out the shorter hairs. Always observe your Australian Shepherd and ensure he remains calm and happy; be careful not to miss any sections. Take this process slowly because it is new to you and him.

12.2 Prepare your Aussie for the bathroom

When it comes to bathing, each breed has different needs. I was delighted that my first Aussie didn't need to be bathed as often as other breeds. At least in that, we Australian owners take a break!

Bathing the Australian Shepherd too often damages his. Too frequent bathing removes the natural oil from his skin.

The Australian Shepherd needs an occasional bath; the first step is to brush him thoroughly to ensure his fur doesn't stick to the bottom of the bathtub.

12.3 How to take care of your Aussie's nails

To best take care of your Australian Shepherd from tip to toe, you should have them trimmed their toenails. Although it may seem like a difficult task, with excellent preparation, you can establish good habits right away that will effectively treat your furry friend.

Start gradually with a pre-finishing exercise as you did for the bathroom. Nail clipping, just like his bathroom, will be something you can do to spend time with your Aussie while saving a lot of money.

When you feel your Australian Shepherd's nails scratching the floor, it's time to trim them. Do not postpone this operation because your dog will slip and get hurt if the nails become excessively long.

Also, if you neglect to take care of his nails, over time, there will be negative consequences on the shape of his feet; it will become painful for your Aussie to run and walk, which is cruel.

You may be scared to cut your nails because you have to use a blade. Read these two secrets carefully to make it easy and safe.

Above all, make sure the dog is relaxed and very comfortable. Next, choose a well-lit spot and put your Aussie in a comfortable position where you can see well; at this point, you have almost reached the finish line.

The dog can sit, lie down, or stand up. Nothing changes for your work. The important thing is that your dog stays relaxed and still, as moving around could cause unpleasant accidents.

12.4 Cleaning the ears

Your Australian Shepherd needs ongoing ear care. Look at his ears and observe them well at least once a week. If their color is red, there is probably an infection, and you need to take your Australian Shepherd to the vet.

Clean his ears continuously. Remove excess earwax so your dog will have excellent hearing and won't have any mites or bacteria in the extra earwax. His ears, if clean, will also smell good.

To thoroughly clean your dog's ears, you will need a soft cloth or cotton wool pads and a suitable ear cleaning solution. You will see that, with some experience, you will be able to clean your Australian Shepherd's ears in minutes.

Go to a pet store or veterinary clinic and purchase a dog-specific ear cleaner. Alternatively, you can use tea tree oil, hydrogen peroxide, mineral oil, or witch hazel.

This procedure is relatively easy; you only have to put a few drops of cleanser in your Australian Shepherd's ear and gently massage the inside to remove ear wax and other dirt. Finally, clean with a soft cloth or cotton swab.

12.5 How to prevent and treat canine cavities

Don't expect your Aussie to brush his teeth himself. Like any other grooming business, brushing your teeth is up to you.

Brushing your Australian Shepherd's teeth might seem fun, but remember that you don't have to mess around with dental problems. Tooth decay and dental infections cause a lot of damage to dogs.

So, if you don't want your Aussie to suffer from dental disease, you must start brushing his teeth from when he is a puppy. Tooth diseases are caused not only by old age but also by a lack of care and cleanliness.

Teeth are not only healed for aesthetic reasons. Damaged teeth and gums, in addition to causing terrible pain, reduce your puppy's ability to chew food.

In addition, bacteria that grow in the mouth can infect the liver, heart, brain, and kidneys.

Hence, a neat and clean mouth helps prevent serious health problems.

Don't expect your Aussie to have fresh breath, but it doesn't have to smell bad either. Get a vet to check for gum disease if you have bad breath.

This will not be an easy task. However, you can use the same gradual support recommended for other grooming tasks, making it less tiring. Move your Aussie's mouth and work until your fingers touch his teeth. Use a meat-flavored toothpaste that you can buy at a pet store or directly from the vet.

Brush his teeth with a small amount of toothpaste on his finger. When you notice, it gets used to it, and use the brush. Start gradually, as you did for nail care, and increase with each session. You will start by brushing a few teeth at a time, and eventually, you will touch them all. Don't overlook your Aussie's gum line and brush gently in a circular motion.

You should brush your teeth every day. If you can't do this, use a tooth scraper at least three times a month to clean the plaque that builds up on her teeth. It is essential to clean the accumulation of plaque because, otherwise, it could become harmful to the back teeth.

CHAPTER 13: Your Australian Shepherd's Health and Veterinary Check-up

13.1 Purchase a healthy Australian Shepherd

The Australian Shepherd is a dog that generally enjoys excellent health. However, some diseases can strike him at any time; for this reason, you need to make sure you buy an Aussie from a professional and reliable breeder.

If you buy directly from a breeder who cares for the health of their Australian Shepherds, it is unlikely that the dog you choose will have hereditary diseases or other types of conditions.

Breeders with long-standing bloodlines and several generations of such bloodlines are sometimes wrong because they no longer test generations as if those diseases could no longer be passed on to the next generation.

Conversely, some conditions may still arise, even if the ancestors did not have an infection. On the other hand, if the disease is sporadic, testing dogs for all possible conditions is unnecessary.

13.2 The most apparent symptoms of the disease

You should pay particular attention to some general symptoms, although they can differ depending on the type of disease affecting a dog. If you notice these symptoms in your Australian Shepherd, you should go to the vet immediately.

Very often, the diseases are sudden, and a dog can get sick in no time. This applies to all breeds, including the Australian Shepherd.

Continuously monitor and check your Aussie by doing a daily health check. The main symptoms that indicate your dog's illness is described in the following few pages.

13.2.1 Lethargy

Although they sometimes rest and sleep, Australian Shepherds are active dogs. But lethargy is not typical. Remember to identify your dog's tiredness, such as excessive exercise or stressful activity. If you don't find apparent reasons, contact your vet.

13.2.2 Problems with urination

Changes in urination frequency and urine color could mean a health problem. Difficulty urinating may indicate certain diseases, while increased urination may be linked to other diseases. If you notice blood in your urine, contact your vet as soon as possible.

13.2.3 Bad breath

Bad breath can be a symptom of an oral problem and other more severe disorders. If you do not identify a specific reason for your Aussie's bad breath, have him checked by your veterinarian.

13.2.4 Skin problems

Always look at your dog's skin; it may have a health problem if it is peeling or a bright red.

If your Aussie scratches a lot, they may have mites, fleas, or even some allergy. So, you must always check for all the reasons that cause skin problems.

13.2.5 Excessive thirst

If you notice your Australian Shepherd taking in large amounts of water even on less hot days, he may be dehydrated or have some form of illness. An Australian shepherd should drink about one ounce of water for every pound of his weight.

13.2.6 Loss of appetite

Loss of appetite is one of the most prominent indicators of something wrong with your Australian Shepherd. If your dog loses its appetite, you need to examine and reprogram the feeding level. But, of course, you should not worry if your dog is picky and skips a meal occasionally.

13.2.7 Frequent drooling

Excessive drooling may indicate a problem. If you notice your Australian Shepherd drooling more than usual, take him to the vet for a checkup.

13.3 Choose a good veterinarian

Choosing a good vet is one of the most important decisions you must make as a dog owner. Comprehensive health care for your pet will help you give him all the necessary care for his health.

In addition, veterinarians generally need to ensure pet owners provide their pets with a very high standard of care and assistance. Another veterinarian's job is to get in touch with owners to instruct them on how to care for and manage their pet's care.

You will not have a happy canine companion if your health is not good. A dog suffering from severe physical or mental problems can become unmanageable and rude.

To keep your Australian Shepherd in good health, you must correctly follow the steps you will find well described later.

Take the time to choose a professional veterinarian who will perform the following tasks:

- carry out annual checks;
- choose a healthy diet for your dog;
- have your dog neutered or spayed promptly;
- inform the owners about problems that can worsen his health.

You should learn the basics of canine **CPR** to save your dog's life in dangerous situations.

Some veterinary clinics specialize in caring for large dogs, while others specialize in caring for small dogs. For your Australian Shepherd, choosing the clinic that best suits his size is advisable.

Choosing a good vet is equivalent to choosing the right doctor for your health. You must ensure your Australian Shepherd gets the care he has needed since he was a puppy. Begin your research by asking other dog owners who their trusted vets are, especially if they are satisfied with how their furry friends are cared for.

Once you have chosen your veterinarian or veterinary clinic, bring your Australian Shepherd to us before the visit. This will get him used to not being afraid of new smells and the new, unfamiliar environment.

13.4 The importance of vaccinations

You will need to take your puppy to the vet within three days of taking it from the kennel. Almost all breeders will give you this advice, and it is a guarantee for you and your puppy.

Have this clause included in the contract with the breeder to ensure that the Australian Shepherd puppy is healthy when entering your home. You could also book subsequent vaccinations with the veterinarian if he is the right age and if it is included in his vaccination schedule.

Scheduled vaccinations may change depending on where you live. In general, the standard vaccinations are as follows:

- Leptospirosis (optional depending on where you live);
- Kennel cough;
- Infectious canine hepatitis;
- Canine distemper;
- Canine parvovirus;

- Canine parainfluenza virus.

In some areas of the United States, a vaccination for Lyme disease, which is spread by ticks, may also be given; however, it is not considered a primary vaccination.

The rabies vaccine is required in every state, usually when the puppy is over four months old.

To fully immunize the puppy, these vaccines must be given several times over several weeks.

Once your Australian Shepherd puppy has completed his vaccinations, he will have to undergo the booster dose at the age of one year. After that, the vaccines will be updated every three years, meaning your puppy won't have to get all the vaccinations again.

13.5 How to detect common viruses and diseases

Even if your dog has never suffered from a common disease or caught a common virus, you need to know the many diseases and viruses that exist to ensure your Aussie's health. Unfortunately, these viruses and infections could harm your dog's health.

Always pay attention to the symptoms of the common diseases, and if you fear your dog has it, contact your veterinarian immediately.

13.6 Allergies as a health hazard for your Australian Shepherd

Dogs could suffer from allergies identically to people. Don't be surprised by this. The Australian Shepherd may be allergic to certain food ingredients or may develop contact or inhalant allergy.

The general symptoms of an allergy are:

- chewing of the paws;
- burning throat;
- diarrhea;
- coughing and sneezing;
- itchy eyes;
- reddened skin;
- ear infections;
- the base of the inflamed tail.

The Australian Shepherd may be allergic to perfumes, cleaning products, drugs, cigarette smoke, hair, feathers, dust, mold, and weeds. Some flea and tick products may also cause allergic reactions, so choose these products carefully.

Also, make sure you only use dog-specific products and substances on your dog.

Dogs are often brought into the vet's office to bite, lick, scratch, and chew their paws or skin. This is caused in most cases by possible allergies or other triggers.

Always ensure that your Aussie never suffers from allergies and that he can live a healthy and peaceful life.

13.7 Spaying and neutering your Australian shepherd

There are many factors to consider when deciding to spay or neuter your Australian Shepherd puppy. Some people do not fix or neuter their puppy because they feel it is wrong and unnatural. However, most dog owners have their pets spayed or neutered.

The number one factor killing dogs and pets in the United States is shelter euthanasia. Millions of dollars are spent each year to euthanize unwanted dogs, and the only way to avoid this tragedy is to neuter or spay your pet. But dogs will be uncomfortable if they are in heat and cannot mate.

Spaying and neutering do not harm your pet's health in the short or long term. However, this is a critical decision you must make with your family. So first, talk to your vet and people who have gone through this experience before.

13.8 Health insurance for pets

It is essential to purchasing health insurance for your Australian Shepherd. With the help of insurance, he can live a longer, happier, and healthier life because he can afford the most effective treatments.

The best idea is to take out insurance when your dog is still small. The insurance will cost more when he gets older because his monthly premiums will be much higher.

CHAPTER 14: Multi-Drug Resistance Mutation - MDR1

14.1 MDR1 genetic mutation

Several breeds of collie origin, including the Australian Shepherd, suffer from this genetic mutation, reacting negatively to various drugs and anesthetics.

For example, drugs that prevent heartworm disease could cause a toxic neurological effect; this happens because if the dog has the mutant gene, he will be unable to eliminate these drugs from the brain naturally.

Some veterinary schools offer a **DNA** test that any dog of collie origin should undergo to identify the mutant gene and to avoid suspicious medications. This is at least until it is discovered if the dog is a carrier of the gene.

Usually, Australian Shepherds are susceptible to drugs precisely because of a mutation in a gene known as **MDR1**. In this case, dogs could exhibit several symptoms, such as depression, seizures, and tremors, which could even lead to death. Unfortunately, the only cure for this condition is prevention; any Australian Shepherd should be screened for the mutant gene.

Vet support with plenty of **IV fluids** can save a dog's life affected by this genetic mutation.

Multi-Drug Resistance (MDR), by preventing the accumulation of toxins that can lead to even fatal seizures, protects the brain by transporting harmful chemicals out of it.

14.1.1 The main drugs that cause problems

Below you can find a list of drugs that cause problems in dogs with the **MDR1 mutation**:

- acepromazine;
- butorphanol;
- emodepside;
- erythromycin;
- ivermectin;
- loperamide;
- milbemycin;
- moxidectin;
- selamectin;
- vinblastine;
- vincristine.

Notify your vet immediately if your Australian Shepherd is sensitive to these medications so you know if he's affected by the **MDR1** gene mutation.

CHAPTER 15: Don't Forget Older Australian Shepherds

15.1 How to adopt an elderly Australian Shepherd

You may also find an elderly Australian Shepherd, although not a very common thing. He could be in a kennel, a dog saved from abandonment, or a dog that the breeder no longer wants to keep.

15.2 The benefits of adopting an older Australian Shepherd

You don't have to train him

Adult dogs are already trained when you adopt them, so you don't have to commit to training your Australian Shepherd to stay indoors.

This depends on the dog, but most Australian Shepherds are already trained before leaving the farm. It is more difficult for a trained Aussie to have negative habits such as continual chewing.

You will immediately receive a lot of affection

The Australian Shepherd breed is considered one of the most affectionate dog breeds. The older Australian Shepherd will be even more affectionate because he will be grateful to his new owner.

You can teach new commands

Even though many adults Australian Shepherds are already trained, you can teach them new commands. An older dog needs time to adjust to his new home, and he may be withdrawn.

A dog takes about a year to adapt to the change. Contact an older dog breeder if you don't want to go to an Australian Shepherd-specific recovery center. You could find it with a web search or with the help of social media.

There are undoubtedly Australian Shepherd rescue groups in your area as well. Beautiful purebred Australian Shepherds regularly end up in shelters, just waiting for a loving family to welcome them.

15.3 The training of the adult Australian Shepherd

You will start more complicated training sessions when your dog is around two years old and is an adult. With patience and persistence, you could teach your Aussie many tricks, commands, sports, and canine exercises; he will be delighted to learn from his master.

You could teach your more advanced adult Aussie to flip over or shake his paws on the opposite side. These are challenging exercises but ones that your clever Aussie can learn.

If you enjoy teaching your Australian Shepherd dog and enjoy learning new tricks or exercises, you may want to consider teaching him a series of hand gestures such as **"Talk"** or **"Commando crawl."**

You could also get them certified as canine therapy to cheer up people who need to spend time in hospitals and care facilities.

Teaching your adult Aussie new tricks and exercises creates respect and confidence and is fun for both of you; also, is a healthy way to exercise the dog physically and mentally, making him a faithful and well-mannered friend.

15.4 Veterinary care for your older Aussie

There are specific veterinary care plans for your older Aussie.

When he turns eight years old, it is advisable to give him a senior exam, which involves some special tests such as **blood tests**, **urine tests**, and other tests. Through these tests, your veterinarian can determine the best care for him, especially in case of illness.

These tests will be repeated yearly to see any changes in your Australian Shepherd's health.

By proceeding in this way, your veterinarian will be able to detect health problems before they become serious.

You can contribute to its care by checking bumps and lumps every time you clean your senior dog. Although chunks of grease or the like are familiar in an old dog, it is best to have your veterinarian examine strange changes in your dog's skin.

A problem found early can be overcome with a high chance for your Aussie to recover.

15.5 Administering Medicines to Your Adult Aussie

Regular exercise keeps muscles toned, reduces joint stress, and prevents weight gain. However, various pain reliever medications can be lighter or stronger if your dog is in pain. Please consult your veterinarian and inform him about your dog's condition. Do not give your dog over-the-counter pain relievers without veterinarian approval, as many medications could be fatal to dogs.

15.6 How to cure your Aussie's arthritis

If your Australian Shepherd has arthritis, remedies such as a heated bed, massage, hydrotherapy, and other treatments could be beneficial. Most dogs will be better off with some of these measures. However, in case of an aggravation of the disease, surgery is recommended.

15.7 The nutrition of the adult Australian Shepherd

Choose foods that have high-quality meat proteins as their main ingredient. Depending on your dog's energy level, give him an amount equal to 3% of his body weight daily. Your adult dog will likely prefer one meal a day, although he will enjoy the morning and evening meals very much.

Be careful when shopping at the pet store; always choose quality dog food.

Conclusion

This book was written with the intent of helping people who are considering sharing their life with the Australian Shepherd. But, first, you must understand if you have the time to devote to this super intelligent dog and if your lifestyle is compatible with breeding a healthy and happy dog.

I hope that after using this guide and learning more about Australian Shepherds and their behaviors, you will feel more confident as a master and trainer. Furthermore, I am convinced that you will be able to make the most of all the information offered.

There are a lot of things you can learn about your dog and the breed as a whole. There will be days when your Aussie will make you angry and impatient and days when you question his intelligence.

But you will soon discover that your belief was wrong and that it was probably your fault. We, humans, are not infallible, and we will always make mistakes.

Don't worry; this is normal when you decide to share your days and spaces with an Australian Shepherd.

We, humans, are fallible, and as such, you will make mistakes again in the future.

There will always be difficult times, but you must be able to cope with them to achieve greater understanding and mutual love with your dog. You need to develop a command on your dog that will become a valuable resource for the future.

You need to be very patient with your dog, and you need to be very understanding with yourself.

If you succeed in this, you will have an excellent relationship and a deep bond with your Aussie that will last for years. A dog brings joy and friendship and improves your health and mood.

Owning a dog requires that you take on the responsibilities of alpha. Therefore, it is up to you to use other resources, such as training videos and books from professionals and other experienced dog owners.

Your sacrifices will ensure happiness and well-being for you and your Australian Shepherd in time.

Made in the USA
Las Vegas, NV
02 November 2023

80044106R00050